Eclectic

COUNTRY

Eclectic
COUNTRY

MARY EMMERLING

photographs by
Reed Davis

GIBBS SMITH
TO ENRICH AND INSPIRE HUMANKIND

TO MY HUSBAND, REG JACKSON;
MY DAUGHTER, SAMANTHA EMMERLING, AND NICHOLAS HALL;
MY SON, JONATHAN EMMERLING, AND ROSY LUM EMMERLING;
AND MY BROTHER, TERRY PAUL ELLISOR.

15 14 13 12 11   5 4 3 2 1

Text © 2015 by Mary Emmerling
Photographs © 2015 by Reed Davis

Published by
Gibbs Smith
P.O. Box 667
Layton, Utah 84041

1.800.835.4993 orders
www.gibbs-smith.com

Designed by Sheryl Dickert
Printed and bound in Hong Kong

Gibbs Smith books are printed on either recycled, 100% post-
consumer waste, FSC-certified papers or on paper produced
from sustainable PEFC-certified forest/controlled wood
source. Learn more at www.pefc.org.

Library of Congress Cataloging-in-Publication Data

Emmerling, Mary Ellisor.
 Eclectic country / Mary Emmerling ; Photographs by Reed
Davis. — First Edition.
    pages cm
 ISBN 978-1-4236-3860-5
1. Decoration and ornament, Rustic. 2. Interior decoration—
United States. 3. Country homes—United States. I. Title.
 NK1994.R87E46 2015
 747.0973—dc23

                            2015014566

CONTENTS

Acknowledgments

I have wanted to do this book for a long time. When Carol Sama Sheehan and I were at *Country Home Magazine* for ten years between 1997 and 2007, we had many long discussions about doing this book together when we left. I am sorry to say that six years later, Carol passed away. This book is for her.

There are so many people that helped put years of memories together. I express gratitude:

To Judy Scanlon, my best friend in Washington, D.C. She moved to New York City for the World's Fair and made one phone call to me asking to move in and be her roommate. I got a job at *Mademoiselle* magazine that lasted thirteen years and produced great friendships that continue to this day, including Sandy Horvitz, Mary Randolph Carter, Andrea Quinn Robinson, and Edie Raymond Locke, our editor-in-chief.

To friends I have met doing stories about them: Martha Stewart, Buffy Birrittella, Duane Michals, Lyn Hutchings, and Mary Higgins.

After thirteen years, I went to *House Beautiful* as decorating editor and met so many friends through the magazine and books: JoAnn Barwick, our editor-in-chief, Joe Ruggiero, Chris Mead, Tricia Foley, Ann Lawrence, Emelie Tolley, Jody Thompson-Kennedy, Peggy Kennedy, Jason Kontos, Katrin Cargill, and Carol and Mark Glasser.

When I opened American Country Store on Lexington Avenue, a wonderful woman, Patti Kenner, walked in and became not only a fast friend but also my best client. Nancy Thomas made great folk art; Lester Breininger made wonderful redware platters that told stories. Bunny Mellon and Jackie Kennedy were just a few of the new friends I was meeting from across the country.

I worked freelance at *Ladies Home Journal* with Kimberlie Waugh, Peter Vitale, and Harry Greiner. After seven years, Chris and I closed the store and opened in Easthampton. I was offered the *Mary Emmerling Country Magazine* and worked with a new group of talented editors: Jill Simpson, Doug Turshen, Kayo Der Sarkissian, Melissa Crowley, and Kevin Crafts.

To the crew at the HGTV show *Country at Home*—Cheryl Masur and Taryn G. Vanderford—and to all the people whose homes we photographed.

To the whole staff of *Country Home Magazine,* where I worked for ten years, but especially Paul Zimmerman, whom we lost to a car accident—I still think of him all the time, and Jen Kopf Zimmerman, who was married to him; Carol Sama Sheehan; Sandy Soria; Catherine Sass Boone; Beth Eslinger; Diana Dickinson; Shaila Williams; Jane Perdue; Lisa Holderness; and Jessica Hundhausen Derrick.

Always, to Jim Arndt, who introduced me to Madge Baird, my editor at Gibbs Smith—what a fabulously talented, smart, and fun editor! To trade publisher Suzanne Gibbs Taylor and freelance book designer Sheryl Dickert.

To Carly Thompson Homer, who helped with editing, typing, and organizing. I couldn't have done it without her!

To Reed Davis, the best, most talented photographer that I worked with at *Mary Emmerling Country Magazine* and *Country Home Magazine*.

The friends from Round Top: Beverly and Tommy Jacomini, and now their family and children, Tommy, Susie, Vivi, and Thomas; Kathy and Harry Masterson, along with their children Kay, Cochran, and Garrett; Joanie Jacomini Herring, along with her husband, Laffa Herring, and their son, Lafayette. They have all given beyond Texas hospitality for forty wonderful years.

To Emma Lee Turney, who started it all and made Round Top famous.

To Susan and Bo Franks, who took over the Original Red Barn when Emma Lee retired and started their antique shows there, and to Ashley Ferguson at Marburger.

To all the wonderful dealers and friends I have met at all the Round Top Antique Shows: Richard and Janet Schmidt, the most talented jewelers at Round Top; Mary Daly, who helped me find houses for this book; Cindy Thorp; Mary Baskin; Bess Baskin; Wendy Riva; Larry Sheehan; Shannon Vance; Vincent Pearl; Danny and Dina Neil; and Nevena Christi of Rocketbuster Boots and Ann Fox.

To wonderful friends and dealers in Santa Fe: Kateryna and Jerry VanHeisch, Nathalie Kent and Jim Arndt, Randy Rodriquez and Donis Quin, Brett Bastien, Jules Barth, Terry Schumeier and Gloria List, and Wendy Lane at Back at the Ranch. In Scottsdale and Phoenix: Jim and Sharron Saffert, Tim and Devin Thompson family, Susan and Doug Rose, Brie Rose, Bev Burch of Willows, Linda Criswell of Bungalow, Alicia Flatin of Bungalow, Billi Springer and Jim Hatfield, Heather Moeller and Sweet Salvage, and Mishawn Roggeman.

And last but definitely not least, to all the wonderful homeowners that let us into their fabulous lives: Dana Aichler, Dot Dimiero and Alexander Molinello, Paige and Smoot Hull, Beverly and Tommy Jacomini, Kathy Jacomini Masterson and Harry Masterson, Linda and Mike Plant, and Rachel Ashwell.

Introduction

People often come up to me and tell me they love my "look." I'm always flattered, but part of me is wondering, "Which one?" Since my first home was published in the *New York Times Magazine* a thousand years ago, my definition of Country has never stopped evolving. Refreshing it and finding new things to add to it are what make it so much fun.

When I was starting out, the classic Country look was popular again, thanks to the Bicentennial, but it sorely needed an update. Being in the magazine business, I always knew where country was going and always had an opinion about where it should go. In August of 1977, *House and Garden* ran a story about my take on country called "A New High: Country Cottage 10 Floors Up." My name was forever linked with that wonderful word.

As I look back, it's a happy blur of eclectic collections and details that warm my heart: striped fabrics, framed American flags, folk art, leopard touches, blue-and-white china, wooden watermelons, watering cans, dried flowers, straw hats, baseball hats, redware, glass kerosene lanterns, chandeliers, English antiques, pumpkins, dried wildflowers, topiaries, linens, shells, bird's nests, sea grass, rag rugs, ladder-back chairs, farm tables, antique rattan, white upholstery, hooked rugs, glass bottles, country blankets, homespun, quilt pillows, gingham, bandanas, barrels of red geraniums, local paintings of lighthouses or beach scenes, and candles—there can never, ever be too many candles.

When I was a little girl, I never could have dreamed of having such a long and crazy career. It's truly been a joy to meet so many wonderful people and help shape a style that I love so much. From New England Country to Beach Country to Cottage Country Style and Country Modern, it always needs a little something new, but it never seems to get old.

Decorating is a way of telling a story. Never stop telling yours. I know I won't.

XOXO
Mary Emmerling

"I am drinking the stars!"

Dom Perignon

I BELIEVE IN PINK.
I BELIEVE IN KISSING,
KISSING A
I BELIEVE IN BEING STRONG
WHEN EVERYTHING SEEMS
BE GOING WRONG.
I BELIEVE THAT HAPPY GIRLS
ARE THE PRETTIEST GIRLS
I BELIEVE THAT TOMORR
AND

MY STORY

I was born and grew up in the Georgetown neighborhood of Washington, DC. It was a time and place so classic I still can't believe it was real: picturesque streets made up of rows of gorgeous townhouses, every home filled with small, intimate rooms, which must be where I got my love for lamp light and adorable, intimate spaces. Everyone knew everyone; even our dogs were best friends with each other. My grandmother lived across the street and had a backyard rose garden. This was back when roses still had their natural scent, and I can still recall that heavenly feeling of walking through her gate.

OPPOSITE: I always do a fun tray or bowl with things I have found or gifts from friends (photos, letters).

LEFT: My parents, Marthena Williams Traynham and Paul Franklin Traynham.

In summer, our family would go to Rehoboth Beach, Delaware, to escape the swamp of Washington, D.C. My life has been defined by certain locales, and the beach is one of them.

I went to college in Virginia and got a job at the Shoreham Hotel in personnel after graduating. It was the place to be at the time, with movie stars and famous athletes coming in the door every day for the Washington Senators baseball games, the Redskins football and, of course, the famous Blue Room. Even the Kennedy men would come by, giving the staff something to gossip about. I'll never forget walking through a hall and Marlene Dietrich popping out of a door to ask me to zip up her dress. That was the day I learned that movie stars don't always wear underwear. My boss's name was Mr. Hollywood, and I worked with him in the beautiful marble lobby doing secretarial duties. There were yearly book conventions—where I got my first glimpse of the publishing world—and a magazine stand, where every summer I bought the August issues of *Glamour* and *Mademoiselle*—all I could afford at the time!

After a couple of years, a girlfriend invited me to go with her to Europe. I knew I just had to go, but I was nervous about losing my job. I walked sheepishly into the hotel owner's office and told him my plan. He looked at me and said, "Young lady, you've been here a long time and worked hard. Here's some money. Here's my phone number in case of emergency. And we'll hold your job until you return." I would have fainted if I hadn't been so excited to go start packing.

I left for a three- month trip to Europe with two girlfriends and a huge smile on my face. We traveled to England, picked up a white Triumph, drove to Copenhagen, Greece, Mykonos Island, Italy, southern France, Barcelona, Ibiza, Paris and back to London. It was amazing to be in so many countries in such a short time. One day, fate decided it was time for me to go to Tivoli Gardens, where I met a cute 6'4" guy from Michigan named John Emmerling. He was meandering around Europe for a few months before moving from San Francisco to New York City. He was writing and selling greeting cards to Hallmark as he went to fund his trip. We met up several times along the coast and took trips together to Barcelona and Ibiza.

After the fun came to an end, he went to New York and I went back to DC. I tried to get serious and be a secretary at a law firm. That experiment lasted six months. I got a great Christmas bonus, but it was not the life for me. That's when I headed back to the Shoreham Hotel. In 1964, my best friend from Washington, DC, Judy Scanlon, called and invited me to take her extra bedroom. She had moved from Washington, DC, to New York City to work for the Ambassador to Jamaica at the 1964 World's Fair. It seemed crazy, but I thought, "I'm not in love with anyone and John is in New York, so why not?" It was the best decision I ever made.

When I arrived in New York, it was just exactly as it was in *Breakfast at Tiffany's*. I had no idea it was so incredibly livable, with a new great neighborhood every ten blocks and a good coffee shop every ten feet. Everyone walked, yet somehow people seemed to move faster than in other places with cars. It was charming, elegant, and fun all at once. One year, there was a subway strike and all the girls switched from high heels to tennis shoes. They were so comfortable they never went back, even when the subway started up again. After work, you'd meet the best people at local bars. If a girl needed a date for the weekend, the secret was to go to the Bloomingdales men's department on Thursday night. I met two guys that way. It was fun and mostly innocent dating.

I lived on 74th Street and 1st Avenue and had a job at Lord and Taylor, until a buyer told me that my taste was too select and I should leave and find another job. (Years later, I did a lecture there for the employees and thanked her for her honesty.) I found another job in personnel at Condé Nast, which is when the seeds of my career were planted.

John and I got married in 1969, just as both of our careers were starting to take off. We started out in a studio apartment on the Upper East Side. My weeks were becoming filled with things I never could have imagined: press trips, three-martini advertising lunches (one white wine spritzer for me) and assignments covering all the country's best furniture, housewares, kitchen and bath and gift shows. We had our first child, Samantha, in 1973 and our second, Jonathan, in 1976.

Living room *Mary and John Emmerling and their daughter, Samantha, share a backgammon game. Modern sofas, covered in white wool, mix with a red-painted American pine cupboard (behind them), a blanket chest with American primitive paintings grouped above it, and an open-shelf cupboard (between the windows).*

Livingroom, fireplace corner *The apartment's 11-foot-high ceilings with open beams and working fireplace provide an ideal setting for a country French desk beside the fireplace, an American patchwork quilt on the sofa and patchwork pillows. Portuguese plates in blue-and-white garnish the fireplace wall.*

Foyer *A Welsh cupboard, circa 1865, displays a selection of ironstone plates and platters. The walls are papered in a yellow plaid.*

Den *The family dines at an English farmhouse table. Behind it stands an English oak settle bench; on the wall a collection of samplers.*

Design By Norma Skurka

Importing the country

Some say it is a reaction to the stereotyped modern interior; others theorize that the simple furniture used on farms and in small towns in 19th-century rural America suit today's relaxed life-styles. Mary and John Emmerling give another reason for the current popularity of country-style antiques. "Life in New York is so frantic," Mary explains, "I like to open the door of my apartment and forget where I am."

The Emmerlings began collecting 19th-century artifacts and farm furniture three years ago while sharing a country house in Vermont with another couple. The cupboards, quilts and ironstone tableware they picked up in antique shops and flea markets (some pieces for a song) were to go into the weekend house they hoped to own some day. At the time they were living in a West Side apartment where the decorative scheme was distinctly contemporary—dark, paneled walls, green velvet sofas, chrome-and-glass tables. But as their collecting continued, their tastes changed.

Eventually Mary and John bought a roomy coop apartment in a prewar building and, selling all their modern furniture, installed their country antiques in the new home. Although the rooms hadn't been altered in any way in 30 years, they were in good condition and needed only cursory patching and new paint.

It wasn't the intention of the Emmerlings to re-create a country farmhouse in a city apartment, but only to borrow the warmth and comfort. The new sofas they bought, for instance, are contemporary. The walls of the apartment are either painted stark white or, as in the case of the foyer and kitchen, papered in bright geometric patterns.

The price of country antiques continues to rise; the Emmerlings were lucky enough to purchase most of their furniture when prices were within their reach. Today, they tend to trade up, selling a table or hutch for one of better quality when they happen upon it. They are aware of the fact that the pieces they bought turned out to be a sound investment. Even their 18-month-old daughter's room is furnished with antiques—a trundle-bed, a painted country cupboard and ladder-back chairs—rather than with, in Mary's words, "a lot of baby furniture that she will outgrow and we won't be able to give away."

Master bedroom *The Victorian bedstead was purchased in Vermont, where Mrs. Emmerling also found the Bristol blue patchwork quilt. Samantha's rag doll from West Virginia graces the bed.*

Child's bedroom *A contemporary green-and-white geometric wallpaper brightens Samantha's room, which is furnished with an antique American trundle bed, a red-painted pine cupboard and ladder-back chairs.*

68

The New York Times Magazine/October 12, 1975 69

The first publicity I got was in 1976 in the Sunday *New York Times Magazine.*

Mademoiselle Days

We had moved to E. 57th Street and lived above Lillian Gish in 1976. I loved going to work every day. I was being paid to be out and about covering fashion, home furnishings, boutiques, and the latest trends. There was a saying, "If you are at your desk, you are not doing your job!" If editors weren't out covering their markets or in the office for meetings, they were probably in the "closet." There was a big closet full of the latest shoes, bags, and clothes. There were also jewelry, scarves, bathing suits, and hats. The closet was to put together outfits for the big fashion features of each magazine. Each issue was worked on at least four months in advance, so we were always aware of up-and-coming fashion statements. Since we were a fashion magazine, we could wear what was on the pages—jeans, riding clothes, short and long skirts, hot pants. Nothing has changed; trends come and go.

Ralph Lauren was just starting his tie business and going into women's wear. He would come up to *Mademoiselle* for meetings. When he did, it was like Annie Hall—we were all dressing like we were Diane Keaton, wearing ties and lots and lots of layers. You could always tell what magazine a girl worked for by the way she dressed.

I was at Condé Nast for thirteen magical years, and I truly would have paid them to work there.

APARTMENT LIVING—A NEW HIGH

1 Country cottage 10 floors up

Country cottage 10 floors up

"Our kitchen is where the family really lives. The old woods and soft, aged colors add a character and friendliness all their own"

House Beautiful Days

One day, one week in 1977 my life changed. Our new apartment on NYC's Upper East Side was photographed for *House and Garden* magazine and appeared in the August issue. The phone started ringing off the hook. I thought it was my friends making calls and joking. The first call was an agent, Gayle Benderoff, who said, "You have a look and you should do a book!" She soon arranged a book deal with Clarkson N. Potter and became my agent for my entire career in New York.

The second call was from *Good Housekeeping,* asking me to interview for the "decorating" position. The third call, and most important, was from JoAnn Barwick, editor-in-chief at *House Beautiful,* asking if I wanted to be her decorating editor. She loved the way I dressed at the High Point Furniture Market. After thirteen years at *Mademoiselle,* it was time for me to move on. JoAnn asked if I wanted to bring anyone. I said yes, Barbara Brooks, my assistant, and also a girl I did freelance work with on food projects, Martha Stewart. We had always talked about doing a book together. She would do the food and I would set the tables.

A Special Flower for Mary Ellisor Emmerling for her contributions to the American Art scene through her books American COUNTRY and the obvious influences in the pages of House Beautiful magazine (June copy just received) from A Texas Country girl, Lorna Francis

House Beautiful let me come to work there, knowing I would also be working on my book. I loved working at *House Beautiful.* Working there made me realize how much I really loved decorating. I realized this is why I loved changing, upgrading, and moving. *House Beautiful* sent me across the country to shoot homes in a variety of styles. We visited modern, country, beach, ski mountain, formal—and I met so many great people and kids; it really started my friendships across America.

While I was working at *House Beautiful* and traveling everywhere to shoot different homes, I was working on the weekends shooting my *American Country* book. I went to *House Beautiful* with the understanding that I could work on the book on my own time. The book came out in 1980.

Martha's Mother: Butter Cookies – TO PRESS
#8 South Turkey Hill
Westport Connecticut 06880

Cream: 1 lb. unsalted butter
Add: 1 cup sugar
     2 Egg Yolks
     Rind grated of 1 lemon
Add: 2 TBS Cognac
     6 cups flour sifted with 1 tsp. baking powder
Chill dough at least 1 hr. before rolling or pressing

OPPOSITE: The apartment photography that changed my life was "Apartment Living: A New High," *House and Garden.*

ABOVE: I received some lovely notes from fans.

LEFT: Martha and I at one of many beach parties in the Hamptons.

Another life-changing event was when I met photographer Chris Mead through Joe Ruggiero. We shot great stories together. One that stands out was "Stately Homes"; they were all over England. JoAnn Barwick came on the trip. We went to lunch at the home of Barbara Cartland, the romance writer. Of course, I had to buy a hat to attend the lunch. It was so fun; her home was all pink.

There were great press trips, business trips, and photo shoots. RCA took us on press business trips to concerts that they had for recording artists such as Frank Sinatra and Elvis Presley, as well as to Disneyland, (RCA helped sponsor the construction of the Tomorrowland ride Space Mountain). We traveled to High Point, North Carolina, for furniture shows and to gift shows for every accessory for the home, to Chicago for the housewares show, and to builder shows and kitchen and bath shows; there was lots of travel to glean ideas for readers of the magazine.

As Chris and I started dating, and then living together, we were photographing houses, people, museums and bed-and-breakfasts. We were going to big antique shows in Pennsylvania and everywhere in New England. We met lots of artists, furniture makers, artisans and craftspeople. It gave us the idea to start a store selling antiques and Americana.

We started with a simple 600-square-foot store in Southampton, Long Island. The store was a huge hit from the day it opened. We sold painted furniture, rag rugs, baskets, pottery, lamps, quilts, ironstone, glassware, primitive paintings and lots of accessories. Anything we loved, we sold.

One day our accountant said, "You all are doing so great; you should open in New York City." That week I was walking down Lexington Avenue and saw a For Rent sign in the window at 969 Lexington. When I got to the office I called the landlord. The rest is history. We opened there in 1983. After a few months, I quit *House Beautiful*

> page 18

From top: Bridgehampton house; Wainscott barn; Santa Fe house (bottom two).

The In-Between Years

We were running the American Country Store on Lexington Avenue in New York City. I was bringing up my adorable kids, traveling all over the country with Chris, doing photography shoots, going to antique shows and big flea markets to buy for the store. I started doing licensing for all kinds of companies like Lexington Furniture, Guildmaster for accessories, Springmade for sheets, Hallmark Stationery and Gerner and Gerner Children's Clothes. I loved traveling to all the stores, all the appearances, and meeting so many people.

Mary Emmerling's Country Magazine

I worked freelance for all the magazines. *House and Garden, Self, American Home, Ladies' Home Journal,* and *Country Living.* While at *Country Living* I got "the call!" John P. Loughlin called and asked if I would be interested in starting *Mary Emmerling's Country Magazine* for the New York Times Magazines! So exciting! Talk about the phone call that changes your life. We started at 110 Fifth Avenue with a small but creative staff. It was like a dream come true. The first issue came out in August of 1993, *Mary Emmerling's Country Magazine—Cottage Style.* We photographed all over the country, working on each issue while planning future ones. We went to press parties, advertising meetings, business lunches and staff meetings. We released seven issues until December 1994, and then the New York Times Magazines were bought by a German company. We were still a start-up magazine and they did not want to spend the $50 million to invest in us. They thought we were a "National Geographic" and kept asking where the giraffes were. The exciting, creative days were over, or so I thought.

Mary Emmerling's Country at Home HGTV Show

In 1994, I got a call from the producers at HGTV asking if I wanted to try out for a show called *Country at Home*. I was already doing my magazine and books and raising my two adorable children, but I went to Knoxville and did my test anyway.

I did that show for seven years—one week per month; we produced thirteen shows at a time and waited to see if we were renewed. We crisscrossed the country with a fabulous crew, having a ball in every town. There was something so fun about being in people's homes interviewing them about how they'd put it all together. It wasn't so different from still shoots; they just called detail shots "B-roll."

The biggest difference in doing TV is the instant change in visibility. I was known a little from books, magazines and lectures before, but after the show aired, people on planes and trains, in bars and restaurants would come running over to say they watched the show. It might get annoying if you're Julia Roberts, but for me it was a great thrill. The people are always so nice. We had a great run, but after a while it was a little too much juggling with my job, marriage, dog and kids.

Magazines have been such a part of my life. I always need to have piles of them close by: new ones, ones I want to go through again, or fun gossip ones. I flip through and then give them to friends. Sometimes I even trade them for free Diet Cokes with the staff at my local lunch spots.

and ran the store. We had famous stars come in all the time—Ralph Lauren, Calvin Klein, Ali Mac-Graw, to name just a few. To this day I meet people who say they came into the store. We were on all the morning television shows, especially the *Today Show*. We did them over and over. We continued in New York City for seven years. Once our lease was up, we closed the doors. I have some great memories, like the time the set designers for the movie *Tootsie* came in and bought all the folk art we had from one of our favorite artists, Nancy Thomas. This is where my love of antiques, and especially country, grew stronger. We attended Brimfield four times a year, plus all the shows in charming Connecticut towns and villages and all parts of New England. We traveled all the way to Maine and back to Pennsylvania. The newspapers

and *Maine Antique Digest* told me where and when all the shows were.

As I started traveling more and more, I would always ask homeowners about stores in their towns and what antique shows I should attend. That is how I started going to bigger shows, like Heart of Country, Round Top and the shows in California—Rose Bowl and Santa Monica. I met so many great dealers and friends. I like to say that I have a best friend in every state.

I opened a store one more time, in Easthampton. It was an old barn right in the middle of the village. When I ran into Ralph Lauren recently, outside of his Madison Avenue offices, we talked for five minutes and he said the nicest thing to me: "Every time I walk into my Easthampton store, I think of you." What a nice compliment!

Country Home

In 1996, I found myself needing a change of scenery from the Hamptons. There's nothing like a breakup to make a small town seem even tinier! New York was always great, but my kids were away at school and it felt like time for something new. My mother had just passed away in Florida after a good, long life and my brother was moving to Phoenix to open up an offshoot of the famous NYC lounge Merc Bar. I told my friend Peter my situation and he said, "Duh! Why don't you move to Santa Fe? You have more friends there than in the Hamptons." Another friend, Lyn Hutchings, had even given me a painting by Carol Anthony that read "To New Directions." All signs were pointing west, so I started my favorite of all activities—packing.

I sold my apartment in New York and bought a house in Santa Fe, ready for new adventures and experiences. I started freelancing for *Ladies' Home Journal*. After a long shoot one day, I took my crew to the Coyote Rooftop Cantina for a frozen margarita. We were talking about going dancing when someone asked me what kind of guy I was looking for. I looked around and said I was looking for someone with a cowboy hat and a cute ass like that cowboy down the bar. That cowboy turned around and it was my Reg. That was 18 years ago, and he's been the man of my dreams ever since. When we're apart, I wear a second watch set to his time so I always know what he's up to. I truly don't know what I'd do without him.

In 1996, I moved to Santa Fe , where I met and married Reg Jackson. While Santa Fe was great for me, Reg got a job in Phoenix, so I began splitting my time, doing the seven-hour drive. One morning, I got another call that would change my life forever. It was from the Meredith Corporation. They wanted Carol Sheehan and me to move to Des Moines and revitalize *Country Home Magazine*. Carol was an old friend and a great writer. She'd also been editor-in-chief of *American Home*. I called her and said I thought we'd be a fantastic team, and she agreed. Meredith said we couldn't have two coeditors, so she would be editor-in-chief and I would be creative director, which was how we both preferred it.

We each arrived in Des Moines on the same day, a city neither of us knew anything about except that we would be calling it home for part of the time for the near future. It happened to be the same day the news broke that Princess Di had been killed. We shared a hotel room and at 5 a.m. got in bed together and watched the news coverage, bawling. Boy, if the people of Des Moines could've seen their newest citizens! But we would be best friends from there on out.

Carol and I went to work on the magazine. We started with Country, cleaning it up and making it more creative to inspire the young kids to start collecting. Then about five years in, we started adding modern chairs, lamps and accessories to country kitchen tables, living rooms and bedrooms to liven things up and differentiate it from other country magazines. We mixed in modern chairs from West Elm or Design Within Reach, the classic '50s kind, which really made us stand out, until everybody started copying us. That's how you know you're on to something!

We wanted to add a fun factor to decorating. I think if you don't have a little fun in your house, you're not going to have fun as a person or a couple. (One thing I learned from Diana Vreeland was the "fun bowl"—a bowl or platter filled with little silly things from everywhere you've been. It can be a little bouncing ball or glow-in-the-dark bracelet or a coin somebody gave you that is special—like the Glenna Goodacre gold dollars I give out to young kids I see that are very well behaved in restaurants. They love it and the parents love it even more.) I would buy tons of the cheap, fun sunglasses in SoHo in New York and give them out to everyone in the office. That way they knew a sense of humor could go along with creative decorating.

We did show houses across the country. The two I remember most were in Grand Central Station, 2001. We had been building the houses and unpacking furniture around the clock for weeks and were supposed to open and have a big party the night of 9/11. That morning I finished up at 6 a.m. and went to my hotel to get some sleep. Reg woke me up at 9 and said to turn on the TV. People were running up Park Avenue. I could barely process something so horrible. I felt so blessed that my kids worked farther north. Everything was closed for two weeks, after which Giuliani wanted the city to reopen. So we opened the show houses and raised $1 million for the firemen and policemen of New York City. People couldn't believe we'd built two houses in the middle of Grand Central Station. One night during rush hour, a man in the crowd stopped and began singing "God Bless America." He was clearly a professional and every single commuter froze and listened quietly to the entire song.

In 2007, the party came to an end. Meredith didn't think *Country* was going to make it. The magazine industry was also beginning its long process of figuring how to deal with the Internet. They let Carol go and the rest of us a couple weeks later. We used every tissue in the office saying goodbye. Now, *Country Home* is a special issue once a year or

twice a year using stock photos. It's a bit painful for me to read. We ran a good, tight magazine for ten years. Great houses, interesting stories, and some of the best people I could ever imagine.

Books

When a literary agent said she thought I had a distinct look and should do a book, we met for lunch, and I dumped a huge pile of tear sheets on the table. Tear sheets were my life at the time. She also saw that I had a huge number of business cards from my favorite antique show vendors. I always asked for one and then had no idea what to do with them, so I kept them all in a directory organized by state. She looked down at all this stuff and said, "This is your book!" We sold it in a week to Clarkson N. Potter, who was looking for something just like it.

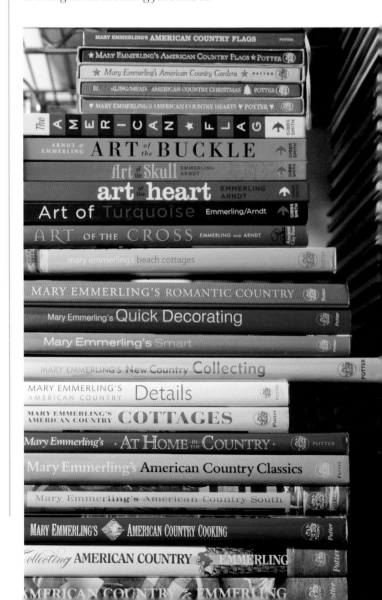

So my first book, called *American Country*, hit the shelves in 1980 and changed everything. At that point, there was only a style called Early American connected with the New England area. I renamed the look to reflect a new style that was all about white walls, big, contemporary upholstered sofas and ladder-back chairs for my 6'4" husband. It probably was the first coining of the term *country modern* and also introduced my penchant for cutting down dining tables for coffee tables. I like them at 23 inches tall instead of the usual 18 inches; this way you can actually use them as a table instead of having to bend down. The book was well received for bringing a dusty old look into the eighties.

In all my travels around then, I started seeing collections everywhere. People made hobbies of finding everything from teddy bears to folk art to pottery. I knew it had to be my second book, and in 1983 it became *Collecting American Country*.

After that, my publisher suggested I go west, and my life changed. I discovered Santa Fe and never wanted to leave. I fell for the beaches in California. Countless places throughout the west touched my soul, and I captured them all in a book called *American Country West*.

Out on the road, each book seemed to lead right to the next one. *American Country Cooking* came next, inspired by all my wonderful new friends who would host and entertain us when we came through town. I continued my countrywide exploration when I did *American Country South*, an exploration of southern history, charm, and decorating with lace and fabrics. They were also famous for their picnics. By 1990 it had been ten years since my first book, and I realized that everyone from my first books had moved to new houses. It was time to revisit them for *American Country Classics*.

In the early nineties, I spent a lot my time in the Hamptons. We were always cooking and throwing huge beach parties, which inspired so many ideas that became *At Home in the Country,* a cookbook.

At this point in my life, I finally realized that one of my true loves was moving itself! After a year or two in a house, my kids would see me pull out the real estate section and they'd start packing for the next adventure. Nothing thrilled me like redoing old houses. And nothing put a smile on my face like empty rooms that needed to be decorated. When I bought four run-down cottages by the ocean in Sagaponack, I had a blast bringing them back to life and shooting them for magazines. I knew there was something so iconic about cozy seaside homes and soon published *American Country Cottages*.

I've often said my life has been told in vignettes and details. I've really made small touches the soul of my decorating style. Picture frames grouped together, wonderful accessories like small bottles on a shelf, little stacks of things I'd find at antique shows and baskets everywhere. I would turn books sideways on bookshelves and display items on top, breaking the monotony and adding character. I banished photo albums in favor of platters filled with my favorite pictures. No one looks at them otherwise! *American Country Details* was about how a home isn't a home without small, loving touches.

After I did another book on collecting, I created *Quick Decorating* for all the people with small spaces who need to put it all together in a week. Easy touches, like using cheap, dark wood peg racks for hanging towels and displaying jewelry. Pulling things out of the back of the closet and finding a way to display them. The book was also for all the people (like me) that live out of suitcases. I even decorate hotel rooms when I check in to make them feel like home.

Romantic Country followed naturally, since I had met the cowboy of my dreams and fallen madly in love out west. Everyone wanted to hear the story, so I thought I'd put in it a book. It was all about setting the mood with white lace, potpourri, and candles—*lots* of candles.

In *Beach Cottages: At Home by the Sea*, I returned to my love of a cleaned-up, simple seaside look. When you're at the beach, you want to be at the beach, not fluffing. I grew up with a beach look that was rattan furniture, hammocks, and baskets full of flip-flops. I made it more distilled and decorated. Peg racks, flowery fabrics, beaded doorways, and light curtains. I never understand why people block out the sun and nature in beach houses. It should be easy on the housekeeping and easy to sweep out on a Sunday night. And no beach house is complete without a dog, outdoor shower with mint planted under your feet, red geraniums in a barrel bucket and baskets of seashells.

In the late nineties, I moved west, splitting my time between Santa Fe and Scottsdale where my brother, Terry Ellisor, was opening the best restaurants the town had ever had, The Zinc Bistro, The Mission, and The House Brassiere. It also let us be closer to Reg's family, who are quite a hoot. I began to do smaller format books with one of my favorite

photographers, Jim Arndt. First was *Art of the Cross*, where I showed off my huge cross collections as well as my friends'. On my trips to Mexico, I'd seek out folk art crosses of silver, wood, and metal. In New Mexico, I started buying rosaries to decorate, with beads varying in sizes, and bracelets with wooden beads and a cross. I love them so deeply and they make me feel protected. And if you've seen my house, I am very protected.

Anyone who knows me knows that since I

discovered the West, I'm rarely seen without some turquoise on. It was always the best conversation starter at parties on the East Coast. So the second book was filled with all my bracelets, pins, necklaces and everything else that's ever been made from turquoise.

Art of the Heart brought together one of the most collected objects I know. Heart stones people find on a hike, heart pins for valentines, bracelet with silver hearts that connect people to their teenage years. My friend Patti Kenner gave me a wonderful bracelet with all silver crosses. She kept a heart bracelet that she let us photograph for the *Art of the Heart* book.

The next was a surprise to everyone, *Art of the Skull*. I swear it started with watching Johnny Depp on Letterman and my long love for Keith Richards. My friend Sandy Horovitz once asked me, "How do you know what's coming next?" I always told her I just keep my eyes open, go people-watching, watch movies. I knew skulls were going to have a big moment, but even I was surprised at how big it was.

When we were shooting, I'd always ask Jim about his belt buckles. He had a collection of thirty jaw-droppingly beautiful ones. I always loved the authenticity of buckles, they're worn by real people with supreme confidence. I even came home from a trade show with one that said "Hollywood" in big letters and Reg said, "That's made by my old stunt guy buddy." *Art of the Buckle* book was released in 2013.

My most recent was the *American Flag* book, photographed by Reed Davis, which I'd been dying to do since growing up in Washington, D.C., where flags were everywhere—embassies, front porches, July 4th parties at the beach. Since then I've always kept an eye out for vintage flags to hang or frame. There's really no wrong way to display the red, white and blue.

There are still so many places and things I can't wait to explore in future books. They help me distill the past but also get me excited for what's next. ◻

40 FACTS ABOUT ME!

BY MARY EMMERLING

- I adore New York City in the spring, when it feels so fresh and Central Park is in bloom.

- My favorite snack is red (only!) Gummi bears. My friends get all the other colors after I pick the reds out.

- I enjoy walking on the beach in the Hamptons.

- My favorite flowers are peonies—all colors. They have a fabulous scent.

- My favorite celebrity meeting was Mick Jagger at Wölffer Estate in Sagaponack, New York. It was just for a few minutes, but magic!

- I love to drink a glass of rosé, Veuve Clicquot champagne, or a margarita—depending on the place or my mood.

- My favorite fruit is a sweet cantaloupe.

- In 1963, I met Marlene Dietrich backstage at the Shoreham Hotel in Washington, DC, and she asked me to zip up her dress.

- I believe in love!

- When I was a teenager in Washington, DC, I was on TV in a debutante special. I kicked my shoes off into the camera and that was the start!

- I am a huge fan of Frank Sinatra, Steely Dan, and Cissy Houston.

- I love to spit cherry pits out a car window.

- My proudest achievements are my two wonderful children, Samantha and Jonathan.

- In 1980, I wrote my first book, *American Country*. It changed my life!

- In 1997, my first TV show, *Country at Home*, premiered on HGTV.

- My two favorite movies are *Breakfast at Tiffany's* and *Out of Africa*.

- I met Reg Jackson in 1996 in Santa Fe. Read my book *Romantic Country* for the whole story.

- I loved skiing in Aspen.

- If I had more time, I would read more and re-read all my favorite decorating books.

- Someday I would love to live at the beach again.

- My favorite thing to bake is Me-Ma Cake. It's my friend Carol Glasser's grandma's recipe.

- My favorite color is black. I call it "the mascara of the home."

- I loved meeting Hillary Clinton at my friend Patti Kenner's house in the Hamptons.

- I can re-watch *Sex and the City* over and over (I always fast-forward through the opening credits!).

- The first 45 record I bought was *Dance Ballerina, Dance* by Vaughn Monroe. I wanted to be a ballerina.

- During high school and college breaks, I had a part-time job working at Lord & Taylor.

- I have a great sense of humor.

- I am currently doing a collection of mixed place settings of vintage English china and dyed antique French monogrammed linen napkins with my partner, Mary Baskin. It's called *The Mary Emmerling Curated Home Collection*.

- I believe it is important to never go to bed angry.

- I saw Elvis Presley, Frank Sinatra, and the Rolling Stones in concerts at Madison Square Garden. Such special times!

- My movie idol is Meryl Streep.

- I love crystal chandeliers.

- I like to snack on Ritz Crackers topped with peanut butter and cucumber slices.

- I love to clean the house listening to the sound track of *Out of Africa* or *Sense and Sensibility* playing on the TV in the background.

- I collect books about black-and-white photography and decorating. Some of my favorites are by my friends, like Mary Randolph Carter, Tricia Foley, Emelie Tolley and Chris Mead, and Rachel Ashwell.

- I love everything Georgia O'Keeffe, especially the museum in Santa Fe.

- My go-to beauty products are everything Kiehl's or anything vanilla!

- I am inspired by my travels to New York City, Bruce Weber photographs, and my children.

- I love Santa Fe, Santa Barbara, Santa Monica—and Santa Claus. What is it about Santas?

- In 1963, I met John F. Kennedy and the Beatles while I worked at the Shoreham Hotel in Washington, DC.

ROUND TOP ANTIQUES FAIR

Round Top happens twice a year, the first full weekends in April & October. Dealers come from all over the country. The population of Round Top when the fairs are not happening is 90! (When I started going in 1980, the population was 76.) Round Top has that Texas pride and the friendly spirit of "you all come back and see us!" The fair is all about antiques, kettle corn, margaritas and BBQ! One dealer I knew from High Point Furniture Market (they are from Atlanta) pulled me aside the first year he did the Round Top show and asked, "Who are these girls—the ones that see each other and start shouting, 'Ahh . . . I haven't seen you since yesterday!'" That's the wonderful Texas spirit that makes Round Top what it is.

ON THE ROAD TO
✕ ROUND TOP ✕

Up and down route 237 you want to—
and should—stop everywhere! For the
scenery, the people, the shopping, and
the absolute best time on the road.

Getting there is half the fun.

Love the miles and miles of ranch fences.

Longhorn steers are everywhere along the country roads.

The American and Texas flags are flown proudly side by side.

AT MARBURGER FARM ANTIQUE SHOW

Mostly outdoors, under huge and smaller white tents. There are formal antiques from all over the world, but mostly Europe and England. Some of the things you will see: pine, painted and primitive furniture, old books, chandeliers, religious objects, baskets, ceramics, furniture and lamps—and ATM machines! Bring your credit card and checkbook.

MARBURGER FARM

Holy Cow

Antique Selfies

WARRENTON

Zapp Hall is the center of the whole show. I love the Field behind the Upper Deck Bar. Work your way towards the Clutter. Stash Style—I love everything Shannon Vance does, from her flannel shirts to her lace dresses and jeans. Across from her is Vincent Peach, a vendor of wonderful pearls and jewelry. Be sure to make your way across the highway to Punkies.

Zapp Hall is in Warrenton. Come a week early
to really fill your truck with treasures!

10 FAVORITE BOOTHS OR TENTS IN ROUND TOP

1. ARBOR (ON HIGHWAY) AND THE BLUE HILLS—both have great furniture.

2. COLE'S—great antiques, air-conditioned building.

3. CLUTTER AREA—just start at Zapp area and walk toward Clutter.

4. EXCESS AREA—opens on first Friday with the best furniture and industrial.

5. LA BAHIA—furniture.

6. MARBURGER—opens Tuesday.

7. BIG RED BARN—original to the Round Top show. Opens Monday.

8. TENTS—

   A, B, and C have the best accessories.

   Tents C and D have the finer antiques; decorators go there first, very inspiring.

   Tent G is an artists' tent, with vintage sculptures, found objects, Around the Bend Willow, folk art.

9. WARRENTON—start at the end and keep walking. At Tree Tops, look for my Santa Fe friend Randy Rodriquez.

10. NEAR ZAPP HALL AREA—
    Stash Style—great T-shirts, clothes, bags.
    Vincent Peach—jewelry and pearls.

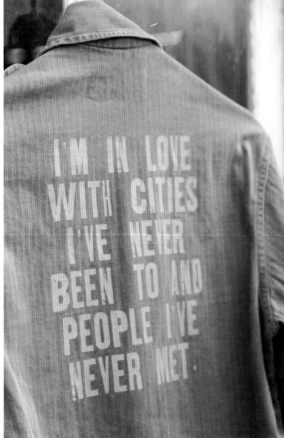

LEFT: Peach has fabulous pearls.

ABOVE: Rio Bravo tent at Warrenton.

ABOVE: Along the highway in Warrenton.

BOTTOM: My favorite jewelry—turquoise.

RIGHT: Light fixtures made from antique world globes. Wish I'd thought of it.

10 FAVORITE THINGS TO TAKE TO ANTIQUE FAIRS

1. HAT—Cowboy hats for Round Top or baseball cap for other events.

2. GOOD WALKING SHOES, cowboy boots or sneakers, and if needed, rain boots.

3. NOTE PAD, PEN OR PENCIL, or cell phone to document and record things you bought or want to go back for. Also, start with a list of what you are looking for and want to buy.

4. GOOD CAMERA or cell phone plus a charger for your phone.

5. PONCHO, raincoat, or small umbrella.

6. PACK OUTFITS for each day and dress in layers. You never know what the weather has in store and you want to be prepared.

7. SUNGLASSES—Very important!

8. EMPTY TOTE BAGS—Size depends on what you are looking for.

9. CHEERFUL, PATIENT ATTITUDE— Always have fun!

10. FRUIT OR NUTS for snacking.

❖ JUNK GYPSY ❖

If you are in Round Top and want new things for yourself or gifts for your friends and loved ones, Junk Gypsy is one of the most fun shops to go to. It is on Round Top 237 just outside of town. They have a pink car that also doubles as the store's sign. You can't miss it! They are famous for their fun T-shirts, kids' accessories, cowboy boots and hats, cowgirl accessories, books, and now sheets and bed covers from Pottery Barn and Pottery Barn Teen.

The BIG RED BARN

EXHIBIT HALL

BIG RED BARN

I love the Red Barn and all the dealers. This barn is where I have been signing books and shopping for antiques the longest. Susan and Bo Franks have grown this show to the size where there are two big white tents in the back with more dealers and European antiques!

Big Red Barn at Round Top is my favorite venue. Susan Franks is in charge of the Big Red Barn, the original Round Top Antiques Fair.

ROUND TOP SQUARE

Richard and Janet Schmidt are a husband and wife team with the finest crafted jewelry in the whole show. I love to see what is new at their tent every time.

There are a lot of tents in the middle of the square. You should go to each one and see what you like. Most of this is new merchandise. I love the flip-flops, the farmer with the homemade preserves and cookies; the sugar cookies are my absolute favorite.

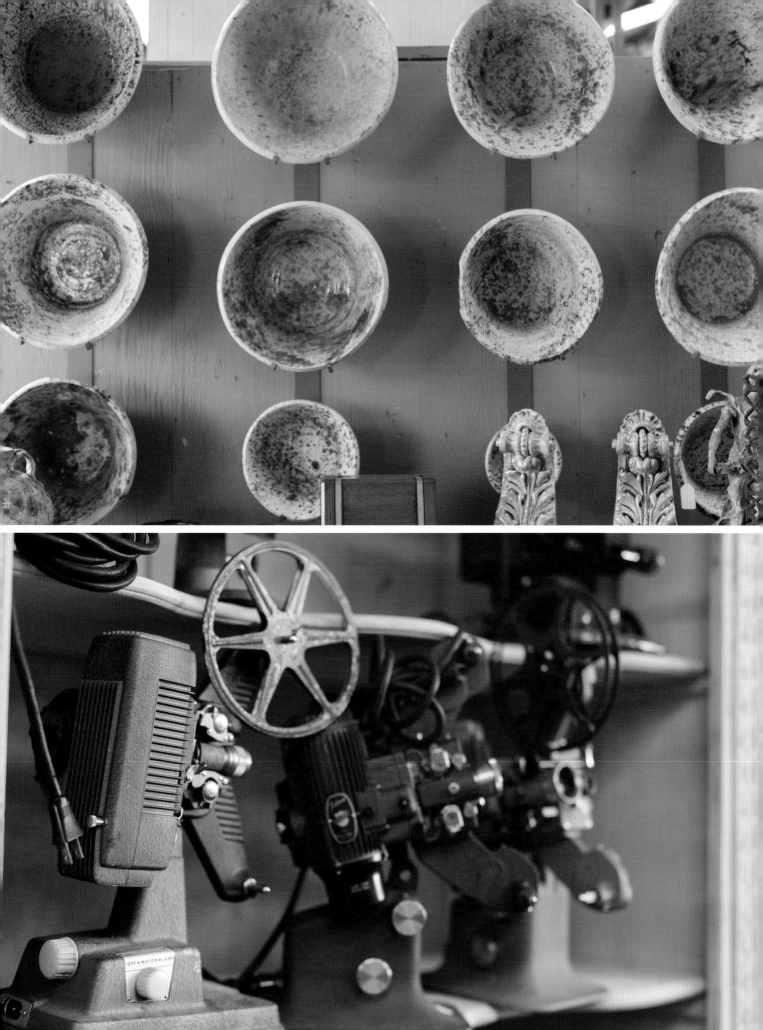

OUR COUNTRY HOME

I can't tell you how many new decorating styles I've tried in my life, but it's probably the same number of times I've moved. A new home is so satisfying because it gives you a brand-new blank canvas to play with. These days you can find my cowboy Reg and me in Scottsdale, Arizona. We live in a community of connected townhouses just a few minutes' drive from my brother Terry's amazing restaurants.

I wanted this house to reflect the eclectic mix I've come to be known for and show off my passion for collecting. It's my classic country style but more about the layers and piles of books, blankets, Navajo rugs, cowboy hats and turquoise jewelry. I always try to incorporate different looks in the same space to achieve that unique eclecticism. Everything can become a decorating layer. Lamps on a pile of books. Pillows on small chairs. Sweaters on wicker stools or trunk baskets. Sometimes you go to an antique show and some great little thing just catches your eye and you have to find a way to display it.

I always start with backgrounds first. I'm a white wall person because I have so many accessories and fabrics that I like to keep the base clean. I decided to do sisal throughout the house this time. It doesn't show dirt, it's easy to care for and it makes the room look bigger. Whenever I do tile floors, I prefer Mexican tile or ceramic, but they can be hard on your back. So now I like wood. Lumber Liquidators will even put a foam under it, which makes it much more forgiving. I also pad under my sisal. ▫

RIGHT: My cowboy hats on a small wooden stool in the den.

LEFT: Up the sisal stairs is a painting I haven't hung and a glitter Eiffel tower.

The sunroom has a great Shabby Chic L-shaped sofa complete with Mexican paintings in the background.

I love white upholstery, but some layered contrast gives it warmth and pops of color where you need it. I'm a sucker for any kind of animal pattern—cow, zebra, or leopard. I always say my closet growls when you open it. When you're collecting, always be sure to think about textures and patterns.

I love slipcovered furniture because it's so easy to wash. Upholstered things are always needing reupholstering and I am a busy lady! Slipcovers are more convenient to clean. You can pull them off and toss them in the washer. You should always put them back on a little damp, it's much easier; when they're a little wet you can mold them down.

If you walked through our house, you'd see that I started collecting even before I wrote books about it. I collect a lot of western things, so I have pieces of antler horns and bullhorns throughout the house or on top of books or magazines. I have every kind of skull you can imagine, collected when I was doing the *Art of the Skull* book. Reg and I both have more pairs of cowboy boots than we can count, so I just let them line the floor around the room. Cowboy hats can be displayed anywhere, from the back of a chair to peg racks. Just don't ever put one on a bed—it's the worst kind of cowboy luck.

OPPOSITE: Close-ups of the sofas in the sunroom with my collection of pillows.

UPPER LEFT: A vintage cowboy hat sits on an antique leather western stool.

UPPER CENTER: Deer horn on top of a magazine.

UPPER RIGHT: One of Reg's cowboy hat collections.

LEFT: Reg's dressing room and some of his favorite cowboy boots. The early 1980s blue cupboard was found in Round Top.

I'm a firm believer in high coffee tables. They used to be very low, and it's back in fashion lately, but all you're doing is hurting your back to put a drink down. I prefer higher so we can also eat off of them if we want to. Height also makes them much better platforms for decorating and showcasing your collections.

Books are ideal for stacking on the floor, by a table or chair, or as a side table. You can never have enough stools; they add height to books or become extra seating when people come over.

ABOVE: The living room is always about TV shows or reading books.

UPPER RIGHT: More books—can't have too many—with pottery, wooden Mexican cross and fringe cowboy gloves.

RIGHT: A leopard ottoman holds more books or can be used for extra seating.

Chandeliers will absolutely never go out of style. They give off great light and diffuse hard shadows so the room has a soft glow. Two of them over a dining table can be a great look. I hang Christmas bulbs from chandeliers around the holidays or sometimes year-round. I even drape Christmas decorations over statues or big crosses around the house. Layering for the different seasons always keeps things fresh.

Something I love, love, love collecting is black-and-white photographs. My go-to is either hanging them on the wall or just placing them on the floor in an empty section along the baseboard.

UPPER LEFT: Antique crocks for wooden spoons.

LEFT: We use the feed bin for a small trash bucket.

ABOVE: We used a six-foot cupboard, cut the top off, fit it around the dishwasher and created our kitchen sink under a beautiful window.

Nothing makes me happier than collecting country furniture. In this house, most of the layout was one big room made up of the kitchen, living room and sunroom. So I took out the old kitchen installations and headed to the Round Top Antiques Fair in Texas. I had measured where the hookups for the fridge, stove and dishwasher were and began buying furniture to do my kitchen fresh. I turned an old flour bin into a trash bin. I used the top of a double-top cupboard to surround the dishwasher. I also dropped the sink into the bottom part of the cupboard. I always set sinks higher than normal because we're tall. In the old days, we were always bending over the sink to brush our teeth. In fact, there's nothing installed to the walls at all in the kitchen; everything is freestanding.

ABOVE: The green pie safe cupboard with sliding doors is used for china, glasses, bowls, storage.

OPPOSITE: A small skinny table is used as the island.

I applied the same technique in the bathrooms, using antique pieces and dropping sinks into them. I even cut long pieces in half and used half in one bathroom and half in another bathroom.

I've always had a strange fascination with all things glow-in-the-dark. Religious figures, rosaries, jewelry—it's all welcome in my house. I love the surprise when you walk in the bathroom at 3 am and a rosary necklace on a peg rack is your night light.

OPPOSITE FAR LEFT: I love my glow-in-the-dark Mexican rosary.

OPPOSITE: My dressing room bathroom. The brown contemporary cupboard was cut in half and used in two bathrooms.

ABOVE: The upstairs sink area. The crosses are from Round Top, Marburger, the Pijnappels'.

LEFT: A silver-painted wood cross from a Mexican church is embellished with a gold heart with rhinestones.

We have two extra bedrooms that we made into dressing rooms, but they're also rooms for relaxing or reading. Reg has his and I have mine. I store all my clothes in mine but also decorate it with wood and silver picture frames everywhere. I used to clean all my silver constantly, but I'm going through a phase now where I just let it tarnish. We should never be afraid to try things that others wouldn't.

ABOVE: I love my dressing room, which also doubles as the guest room. Beds need to be real comfortable, with cotton or linen sheets and lots of pillows. Isn't it inviting?

UPPER RIGHT: Detail of the crosses in the bathroom.

RIGHT: My cross collections stretches throughout the entire house. I bought this cross in Paris.

Reg's dressing room, with his collections of antique cameras and belt buckles. Keeping collections organized in baskets, groupings, or stacks is essential to preventing a cluttered look.

TOP: Looking from the staircase into the upstairs bedroom. A two-piece black 1920s cupboard is filled with books and favorite antiques.

ABOVE: A peg rack holds summer straw hats, bags and scarves.

When we moved in, the closets had horrible metal doors, so at Round Top I found some wonderful old gray shutters to replace them. The contractor almost killed me after making him take them apart and retrofit them. Despite the difficult task of installation, they absolutely make the room.

One classic trick I employed a lot in this home is replacing new doors with vintage doors. Nothing will give the place a more instant connection to the past. Doors can be the soul of a home, especially when they have weight and character.

One of the fun surprises guests discover is on the back of our front door; it's entirely covered in old milagros. People never see it when they arrive, but they always notice later and it makes them smile. (Previously I used them on a headboard.) Milagros are religious folk charms used in Mexican churches in a similar way as candles. If someone had fallen ill or had broken arm or leg, a person would put that milagro in the church as a get-well prayer.

In the front of the house, I have a big metal cross I found in Round Top and a skull in the middle of the cactus garden, so everyone who drives by knows what I collect! During my childhood summers at the beach, every home had a flag, so I display the stars and stripes in abundance, outside and inside. They're just such colorful and iconic decorations. I'll even frame antique flags.

OPPOSITE: A large galvanized cross is in the front garden with the American flag. ABOVE: Flags are another item seen throughout my home. I even have flag towels laid out by the pool. UPPER RIGHT: A close-up of the skull with bandanas. LOWER RIGHT: My Texas longhorn overlooks colorful Mexican pots full of cacti in the backyard.

Our backyard is contained by a pink stucco wall inspired by the Mexican architect Luis Barragan's famous pink walls. We put in a small turquoise pool for cooling off on hot nights. Orange trees that came with the property mean a lot of picking, but nothing beats fresh-squeezed orange juice. I have set against the wall a big mirror framed in old driftwood I found in Santa Fe. In the eighties, I photographed one just like it in the Key West garden of the famous designer Angelo Donghia. It always stuck with me as a fantastic idea, because it gives dimension to a garden and looks like a pathway.

When I was shooting this book, I found a giant, inflatable yellow duck for the pool. A lot of people see it and think I've lost it, but it makes me giggle, so I couldn't care less.

OPPOSITE: Mixing textures keeps my décor interesting. In the backyard, I have a Mercury ball and a basket of shells atop my blue farm table.

ABOVE: A driftwood mirror reflects the whole backyard.

I love collecting personal items that people make for me, especially my children, Samantha and Jonathan. I leave the things out so I can feel like my children are always here. A favorite is a book they made for me called "Momisms" – a handmade record of the most ridiculous things I've said after a few margaritas, and the things I do that they think are crazy, like not allowing trash to be in trash baskets. The minute there's trash in there, it's time to empty them.

After so many trips to Paris, I just had to start collecting Eiffel Towers. I started with little metal ones, then bigger ones, until I finally found one covered in crystals that barely fits in my house. I saw it for sale by a friend at a gift show and loved it. She later called me up when she was closing her store and said she had two in the warehouse. I bought one and my brother came over to buy the other for his French restaurant called the Zinc Bistro. These days, it's his customers' favorite place to have their picture taken.

I'm a champagne girl, but I love having a cocktail bar for guests. Mostly because it's another thing to decorate. I collect certain styles of glasses to give the bar a distinct look. I'm very big into the non-wine glass. I like little antique ones I buy on the road. I'll add antique bottles between the liquors, maybe with plastic rosaries from Mexico on them.

I collect a lot of hearts that I put on top of books with interesting titles that have to do with celebrating.

One of my newer collections is crowns. A lot are just for decorative purposes, but I also collect them for people's birthday parties. I try to always remind people that decorating doesn't need to be fussy or pretentious. The whole point is to color your life with stories and keepsakes.

One big thing going on now in collecting, especially at Round Top, Marburger and Red Barn, is mixing industrial with country. It feels very fresh to mix wood with metal or chairs from the fifties with a country table. The eclectic look is so big now, and I think it's here to stay. The industrial element cleans up the country look and makes it so much more contemporary and exciting.

The best part of collecting so many things is that it turns antique shows into fun adventures. You just never know what you'll find, and you can't wait to find it. I've never smoked a day in my life, but I found a Lucky Strike cigarettes painting and it's one of my favorite little paintings ever. I call these finds my little gems. They make my life feel more intimate and joyful. I say if it's not a happy memory, sell it. But if you love it, keep it out and look at it every day.

TIPS FOR TAMING
ECLECTIC
STYLE

- Wicker tray baskets for flatware.

- White ironstone pitchers for paper towels, wooden spoons, displaying flowers or lemonade.

- On the floor—sisal, sea grass or area rug; or if you own your home, wall-to-wall.

- Curtains—double width so they are full, long, and puddling.

- In bathrooms—white bath towels, hand towels, washcloths, rug, shower curtain and liners. Do two each of curtains and liners to look fuller.

- Wicker baskets for flip-flops, toilet paper, scarves, paperwork, shoes.

- Dimmers in every room.

- Lamps, always 3-way bulbs.

- Tags off—yes, even pillows and mattresses.

- Jewelry as décor—hang necklaces on a peg rack, cabinet handles and doorknobs. If it is out, you will remember to wear it.

- Two chandeliers over a long dining table.

- Industrial racks in the laundry room or garage for storage: extra garden supplies, gift wrap, gifts, seasonal items, entertaining items such as pitchers and platters, and beach baskets.

THE 5J FARM

⊹──◈──⊹

In 1970, Beverly and Tommy Jacomini purchased a piece of land, as well as an 1857 farmhouse that they moved, in two pieces, to where it rests today. The 5J Farm was created for the enjoyment of the Jacomini family and friends.

Beverly, a well-known Houston designer, has been attending Round Top since its inception. I was introduced to her during my first trip there in 1980. When asked what her favorite piece or purchase is, Beverly replied, "The linen press that's in my stenciled room at the farm. The antique dealer is no longer at the show, since it was bought so long ago." Of all the pieces she has collected over the years, an early Texas bed in her son Tommy's room upstairs and her bedroom wardrobe are two of her favorites as well.

After all these years and even with the addition of a new kitchen, the Jacominis' home is very much the same as it was the day I first walked in. Some things never change, and I like it that way.

The living room is centered around a beautiful fireplace and mantel that are original to the home, creating a cozy and tranquil atmosphere. The walls feature beautiful stenciling at the top. Quilts are a theme in this home; some are framed as wall art.

The green paint is original to the 1857 farmhouse living room.

UPPER RIGHT: Another seating area at the end of the living room, with a country sofa.

RIGHT: This painting has been hanging over the fireplace for 40 years. The early American landscape is framed in a faux-painted wood frame.

OPPOSITE: The stove was originally in a separate cook house. When Beverly designed a kitchen for the home, she made place for the antique stove. Yes, it still works!

As farmhouses of this era did not contain kitchens, Beverly created the kitchen to include the antique stove. Hanging copper pots, antique cookbooks and baskets provide a warm and welcoming environment. Beverly expanded the kitchen in 1993, just in time to host her daughter Joanie's wedding.

The area that is now the dining room was used as a hay barn after the previous owners moved to a new home. The stenciling adorning the walls was therefore preserved. The beloved table and pie safe are early Texas pieces.

The master bedroom displays country tables and lamps
from Round Top and a unique headboard fashioned
from fabric hung as a curtain.

OPPOSITE: The couple's bed is country
comfort. The curtain headboard and
pillow fabric in soft pastel promotes rest.
Beverly found all the country tables and
lamps at Round Top.

LEFT AND ABOVE: Their dogs, Sophia
and Osso, have their portraits taken in the
master bedroom.

The upstairs guest room is filled with wonderful pastel quilts that complement the soft blue painted walls.

The porch was added when the house was moved and later screened in. It is filled with twig furniture that Beverly painted white to provide some coolness in the hot summers.

OPPOSITE: A carpenter's work table now holds Texas plants.

ABOVE: A carved white swan sits on the porch zinc dining table.

RIGHT: A heart twig side table.

There is a charming log cabin on the farm's property that Beverly uses as her art studio.
She loves to watercolor.

Tommy's hobby is flying his model airplanes, which he paints by hand. He enjoys taking
his dogs down to the flying field on the farm so they can watch him fly.

LA ESQUINA FARM

K athy Jacomini Masterson has been a Houston designer for almost twenty years. She began her career working with her mother, Beverly Jacomini, at Jacomini Interior Design, Inc., and started her own business, KJM Design, in 2008.

Kathy was just two when her parents bought and created the 5J Farm. Kathy could barely see over the weeds when she would run around the property enjoying childhood weekends and vacations at the farm with her sister, Joanie, and her brother, Tommy.

La Esquina Farm, within the grounds of the 5J farm, was conceived and built by Tommy Jacomini Jr., and his wife, Susie. Kathy inherited this beautiful home when Tommy and his family passed away in an untimely accident. Kathy's home is serene—comfort mixed with industrial accents. The open kitchen and dining area feature drop lights, stone walls and a large island that houses a sink with industrial faucets. The antique dining table is made from old boards. ▫

ABOVE: Kathy and Harry have kept the memories of her brother, sister-in law, niece and nephew alive while making La Esquina a second home for their own family.

LEFT: Drop lights give the high-ceilinged open kitchen and dining area a human scale. The chairs are a great mix. Zebra rugs are very popular in Texas homes.

You can feel the sense of family, history and home as soon as you enter the doors of this tranquil and lovely space. Kathy and her husband, Harry, along with their children, Kay, Cochran, and Garrett, have done an amazing job of making new memories while honoring the memory of her family.

Looking over the kitchen island towards the living room.

Two French-style chairs and a wine-tasting table found at the Arbor in Round Top delineate the dining space from the living area. This is a great place to socialize, relax and play a game of cards.

Just behind are two sumptuous sofas surrounded by bookcases purchased at Round Top and filled with beautiful family photos and books from friends.

The bookcases in the living area hold a lot of country accessories bought at Round Top.

The powder room off the kitchen has a fabulous hanging crown light fixture. This is one of my favorite pieces in the home. The sink is chiseled stone with a brass faucet and gold wood-framed mirror.

A large window in the office area off the master bedroom provides light to perfectly showcase Tommy's architect's drawing table that is now Kathy's desk.

One of the children's rooms is home to a pair of raspberry velvet oval chairs, another great Round Top find. They are placed in the middle of the room in front of a window that fills the room with brilliant light.

The guest bedroom carries on the style of the rest of the house with an iron side table, stone lamp and large comfortable pillows. More lamps, family photographs and memories fill the room.

Writing table in the guest room.

The industrial yet homey feel continues into the master bedroom, where there is an iron canopy bed, and the master bath, which has a bathtub in the middle of the room, with an open shower to the right. The stained concrete floors complement the relaxing bathroom.

ABOVE: Master bathroom. The toilet is on the back left of the tub and the shower is on the right

NEW COUNTRY DREAM

❖◇❖

Linda Plant has been attending Round Top since the early nineties and never misses the spring show. The wild bluebonnets that bloom all along the highways make it a truly magical time to visit.

"Some of my fondest memories, and something I always look forward to, are the Tuesday mornings the first day of the Marburger show." Linda says that waiting in line at Marburger year after year with dear friends is one of her favorite times. The anticipation and excitement are contagious. "I literally go to every booth and show and love every minute!"

Linda and her husband, Michael, built their home in 2012. It's a country dream—soft, inviting and beautiful. Beverly Jacomini was the designer, Barry Moore the architect and Laniel Wolff the builder. Linda says, "They were so important in making our house beautiful, especially Beverly."

OPPOSITE: French-blue shutters, framed antique prints.

RIGHT: Crosses bought in San Miguel.

In the kitchen is an old wooden shelf that Linda rescued from the fields, believed to have come from an old hardware store. It's now in her pantry, holding all her cookbooks and wine. Along the walls are custom-made wooden shelves to display the Plants' beautiful pieces, such as wine glasses, serving dishes, and all the ironstone pitchers they have collected over the years. "The graceful shapes and creamy color make me happy," Linda says.

PURE BUTTER

Above the kitchen hangs a glass pendant lamp from Brown in Houston. Across from that is a chandelier from Circa Lighting, above her dining table, which was made by Dave Lennard, a vendor at Excess Field in Round Top. The table is an old pine door trimmed in pressed tin, looking rustic and fabulous!

In the living room are countless finds from Round Top, displayed proudly among pieces from all of Linda's travels. In front of her two matching mineral-green sofas is a metal coffee table made out of an old farm tray found in Round Top a few years back. A favorite of mine in her home is her set of French-blue shutters on the entertainment wall. The sofa table behind the sofa is another Round Top find.

An additional seating area in the living room holds two oversized chairs complete with ottomans. All fabric is from Rachel Ashwell, bought at the Prairie in Round Top. A large painting of a cow is one of Linda's favorite pieces. The hall is adorned with nine prints that came out of a big book of pictures that Linda and her friend Mary Daly found at an antique show in Columbus.

The home has two guest rooms, one for boys and one for girls. Both rooms are covered in bead board and have twin beds. The boys guest room has a bookshelf that was made as a surprise gift for the couple by their contractor from the leftover wood. The girls guest room displays a vintage dresser from Round Top with a large vintage lamp on top.

The master bathroom has a rare antique ladder from Round Top used as a towel and accessory rack. The master bedroom has a custom headboard by Eva's New Design covered with a Pottery Barn quilt. At the bedside is an antique chest purchased at Marburger. A large painting of Linda and Michael's six-acre farm hangs above a monogrammed settee.

Customization and sentiment are such important traits in a home. In the sitting room, art and objects are arranged in a vignette around the French secretary desk. To the right is a painting of a black lab that reminds Linda of their dog Millie.

OPPOSITE: Sitting room.

ABOVE: Mother's secretary desk.

LEFT: I love the metal box that holds rain boots.

THE VINTAGE ROUND TOP

Paige and Smoot Hull live in Houston and became antique dealers who, like most dealers, had too many antiques. They also had too many ideas of what to do with them all. So in 2011, they decided to purchase a fourteen-year-old farmhouse in Round Top and used all their antiques and ideas to open a fabulous bed-and-breakfast. They call it The Vintage Round Top.

The Hulls developed a signature style called modern vintage, which combines clean lines with industrial and vintage touches. What a great idea! The Hulls have been attending the Round Top shows for fifteen years now. Although both shows are amazing, they prefer the spring show. One of their favorite memories was during the Marburger Farm fall show in 2013. They had just returned from Provence, where they had gone on a buying trip. They set up their first booth and it was the beginning of a new chapter in their lives.

Of all the antiques they have acquired over the years, they definitely have their favorites. They have a trunk that is used as a coffee table, a large birdhouse and, of course, Smoot's grandfather's desk, which has a place in the bedroom.

Gail Rieke had the idea first, but this wall of antique suitcases was designed by Paige and Smoot. They put the suitcases on the floor to see how it would look. A carpenter made a frame for the suitcases to fit in. Only the fronts are used; the backs have been cut off.

Love the numbers on the steps to the loft bedroom

Smoot told lamp artist John Petty to make it look like a spider.

Their dining room table was originally used by a traveling carnival. The Hulls often smile thinking about who might have sat at that table before them. The bearded lady? A sword swallower? Or the tallest man in the world? Every piece has a story, and when the story is unknown, it is all up to one's imagination.

The back living room sofa that doubles as a bed sits on pallets. The headboard is made from an antique wood door. The French-type pillows, bought online, are feed sacks. Feed sifters, above, are metal and early 1900s; the fringe is burlap. The ottomans are new, made to look old.

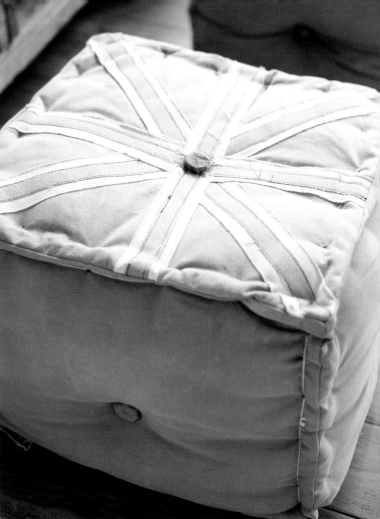

The ceiling wood is from Habitat for Humanity.

OPPOSITE: An antique chair painted white was found at Round Top. Tin angel wings were added.

ABOVE: The large mirror leaning against the wall serves to visually enlarge the space.

Detail of an iron headboard in the loft. It was once a garden trellis. The glass lamp bases are filled with bocce balls.

A metal bed spring is now a sort of memo board for a sign-in desk for guests. The old typewriter and spice tins for paper clips were collected at Round Top. The table is from Uncommon Objects in Austin.

Paige and Smoot have a space at the new Round Top Vintage Market, right across the street from their Vintage Round Top Bed and Breakfast.

OPPOSITE TOP: A primitive picnic table and benches on the side porch with an old tin mailbox.

OPPOSITE BOTTOM: Wicker furniture found at Red Barn, right up the road.

LEFT: Smoot and Paige coming home.

LEFT BOTTOM: A primitive nesting box for hens.

THE BARN

Dot Dimiero is a talented interior designer along with her partner and daughter, Dana Aichler. She also partners with Alexander Molinello and Dana Aichler to publish the international interior design magazine *Antique Shops & Designers*. Dot owns an antique shop and design studio called Twenty Six Twenty, located in River Oaks, Houston. She first attended Round Top over thirty years ago and has watched it evolve every year since. She loves catching up with old friends and finding unbelievable, one-of-a-kind antiques, never forgetting to stop by Marburger, the Arbor, and Excess. At one show she found a huge religious canvas for a steal. It's one of her favorite pieces in the Barn, which is a second home shared with her life partner, Alexander Molinello.

The Barn is a one-story metal structure that feels like a classic American barn. It has 24-foot ceilings and a wall of steel-frame windows. It is filled with European antiques and white upholstery. Dana also contributed to the interior design of the Barn. One of their favorite finds throughout the years is a large gold crown from a church in France that hangs above their Belgian farm table. Mismatched chairs lend a visual liveliness. The living room displays a large pale yellow cabinet along the wall, with stained concrete floors beneath. Many of the pieces were found on their adventures at Round Top.

Funky painted primitive chair with a red/beige linen fabric. The unique painting of
freesia and fruit has paintings within the painting.

In the bedroom, a large chaise from Sweden sits below a Venetian religious painting on wood. Across from the bed is propped a wall-size mirror that has been encased in an antique Italian door frame. White linens give the room a crisp, clean feeling, while antique shutters serve as a creative headboard.

UPPER RIGHT: Big framed mirror.

RIGHT: A three-drawer French cabinet; lamps are from Round Top.

Master bathroom with double sink in an antique cupboard.

Slipcover chair in master bath.

The bathroom displays another beautiful Italian mirror and a large painting, an original Molinello, over the freestanding tub.

In the art studio, several paintings cover the walls. It is a mix of collected pieces and works done by talented friends, family and, of course, by Dot and Alexander. A large religious painting hangs on the wall.

Books of art are stacked high; paints are collected in a large bowl and brushes in tin cans, just waiting for creative inspiration. While vintage pieces, white linens and original artwork fill the Barn, there is just a hint of zebra here and there, on a chair and a small footrest. The loving mix of art, culture, simplicity and beauty make the Barn incredibly inviting.

A wall tapestry, cowhide on the floor, and leather-covered ottoman add not only sophistication but also warmth to this space designed for relaxing. In another seating area, toss pillows on an antique bench make an inviting place to discuss the art.

OPPOSITE: Barn doors from France.

ABOVE: A capital turned into a table is a great conversation piece.

PRAIRIE COUTURE

The Prairie dates back to the mid 1800s. Rachel Ashwell purchased it and opened a beautiful bed-and-breakfast in Round Top in 2010.

There are five little cottages decorated in Rachel's classic Shabby Chic. There is also a store on the property where you can buy items and take the signature look home. In addition, there is a community building with a kitchen, dining room, and living room where the guests gather for breakfast and conversation. A stay at The Prairie is truly a treat.

OPPOSITE: Rachel Ashwell buys a lot of vintage items and ships them to her Shabby Chic stores.

ABOVE: The road to The Prairie.

The Shabby Chic sheets are beautiful and soft. The chandeliers pull the entire bedroom area together.

LEFT: An oriental rug brings richness to the room, while stencils underneath add visual texture.

ABOVE: Love the detail of the peach roses.

A pedestal sink in one of the guest rooms.

I love going to visit Rachel here at The Prairie.

OPPOSITE, BELOW: Entrance to the office at The Prairie.

LEFT: The windmill at The Prairie.

BELOW, LEFT: Another building on the beautiful property.

BELOW: Rustic fencing.

Resources

Aaron Rambo
3433 W. Alabama
Houston, TX 77037
713.522.9191
www.foundforthehome.com
aaron@foundforthehome.com

Antiquaire De France
Henri Delclaux
115 Perimeter Center Place
Atlanta, GA 30346
404.279.0478
www.antiquairedefrance.com
antiquairedefrance@yahoo.fr

Arbor International
P.O. Box 5441
Alvin, TX 77512
281.388.1075
arborantiques.com
roundtop@arborantiques.com

Around The Bend
Willow Furniture
Rick and Denise Pratt
7883 Cleveland Rd.
Wooster, OH 44691
330.345.9585
aroundthebendwillowfurniture.com
willow@sssnet.com

A. Tyner Antiques
Angie and Hugh Tyner
425 Peachtree Hills Ave., Ste. 13
Atlanta, GA 30305
404.367.4484
www.swedishantiques.biz
atynerant@gmail.com

Avery Taylor Designs
Dianne A. Taylor
3719 W. Creek Club
Missouri City, TX 77459
281.723.9645
dianneaverytaylor@yahoo.com

A Wilder Place in Time
2213 Lakeway Terrace
Flower Mound, TX 75028
972.342.8776
Lindat.Wilder@verizon.net

Barbara Trujillo
2466 Main St.
Bridgehampton, NY 11932
631.537.3838

Big Red Barn
Original Antique Fair
Susan and Bo Franks
475 S. Hwy 237
Round Top, TX 78932
5 Miles North of the Round Top Square
512.237.4747
info@roundtoptexasantiques.com

Bootitude
Christy Solomon
219 Clark Rd.
Dallas, GA 30157
404.895.8483
christysolomon@mindspring.com

Bungalow Furniture
& Accessories
15330 N. Hayden Rd., Ste. 120
Scottsdale, AZ 85260
(480) 948-5409
linda@bungalowfurniture.com

Carola Pfau
Textiles
512.452.4454
http://pfau-shop.com
carolapfau@gmail.com

Cottonseed Trading Company
Marsha and David Smith
381 Wildwood Ln.
Jacksonville, AL 36265
205.613.0235
cotonseedtradingco@gmail.com

E. Lawrence, LTD.
1799 Marietta Blvd. NW
Atlanta, GA 30318
404.355.9226
elawrenceltd.com
elawltd@bellsouth.net

Elephant Walk Interiors
and Antiques, Inc.
Ender Tasci
835B Bennett Rd.
Orlando, FL 32803
407.897.6022
www.elephantwalkantiques.com

Eneby Antik
Doug and Carina Jenkins
404.512.4007
enebyantik.com
info@enebyantik.com

French Laundry Home
2501 Mendenhall Rd.
High Point, NC 27263
336.883.2680
www.frenchlaundryhome.com
CSR.frenchlaundryhome@gmail.com

French Touch
Elyan Reboul
619.990.3725
Frenchtouch10@ymail.com

Found
Kristin & Dan Alber
7131 W. Ray Rd. #13
Chandler, AZ 85226
480.733.6863
foundbydomesticbliss.blogspot.com
foundbyab@me.com

Gunslinger
Melissa and Jim Benge
1107 Cypress St.
Bandera, TX 78003
830.796.7803
Gunslingerofbandera.com
melissadesign@aol.com

Leah Martin
201.844.7966
leahmartindesigns@gmail.com

Leftovers Antiques
3900 Hwy. 290 W.
Brenham, TX 77833
979.830.8496
leftoversantiques.net

Lizzie Lou
Mary Lou Marks
107 Main St.
Round Top, TX 78954
832.372.7217

Lolo French Antiques
Laurent Gouon
3101 3rd Ave. S.
Birmingham, AL 35233
205.323.6033
www.lolofrenchantiques.com
info@lolofrenchantiques.com

Mae Dell and Elwood Hanath
5059 Hwy. 290 W.
Brenham, TX 77833
979.836.2889

Marburger Farms
2248 Texas 237
Round Top, TX 78954
800.947.5799
roundtop-marburger.com

Marc Navarro Gallery
Jose Inez Navarro
812 Canyon Rd.
Santa Fe, NM 87501
505.820.9266
casanavarrogallery.com
joseinez@marcnavarrogallery.com

Melissa Benge Collection
2823 N. Henderson Ave.
Dallas, TX 75206
214.821.1777
www.melissabengecollection.com
melissadesign@aol.com

Memorial Antiques and Interiors
8719 Katy Fwy.
Houston, TX 77024
713.827.8087
www.maihouston.com

Michelle Garcia
809 Hunters Hill Trace
Old Hickory, TN 37138
615.870.8163
mgarcia@peachpearl.com
www.peachpearl.com

Munday & Munday Antiques
Makala & Sandy Munday
618.406.4657
mundayantiques.com
Munday37@hotmail.com

Nancy Fishelson
310.508.1446
Nancyfishelson.com

Nathalie
503 Canyon Rd.
Santa Fe, NM 87501
505.982.1021
nathaliesantafe.com
nathaliesantafe@gmail.com

Nomadic Trading Company
619 Foster St.
Durham, NC 27701
919.688.2850
www.nomadictrading.com

Old Glory Antiques
12401 Washington
Burton, TX 77835
303.798.4212
oldgloryantiqueshome.com

Old World Antieks
Round Top Antiques Fair—Blue Hills
1701 State Hwy. 237
Carmine, TX 78932
832.268.4357
www.oldworldantieks.com
oldworldantieks@gmail.com

On The Veranda
4748 E. Indian School Rd.
Phoenix, AZ 85018

602.955.8690
ontheveranda.net

Paragon Antiques
Melissa Estock
205.532.3425
www.paragon-antiques.com
miestock@aol.com

Peter & Shirley Pijnappels
30 Kenowa Ave.
Casnovia, MI 49318
616.675.5808
pijnappels@aol.com

The Prairie
5808 Wagner Rd.
Round Top, TX 78954
979.836.4975
info@theprairiebyrachelashwell

The Raven
1225 Cerrillos Rd.
Santa Fe, NM 87505
505.988.4775
www.recollectionssantafe.com

Reworks
2401 Thornton Rd.
Austin, TX 78704
512.330.0825
questions@reworks-works.com
www.reworks-works.com

Richard Schmidt
118 N. Washington
LaGrange, TX 78945
979.968.5149
richardschmidtjewelry.com

Rio Bravo Trading Co.
Randy Rodriquez
411 S. Guadalupe St.
Santa Fe, NM 87501
505.982.0230
riobravotradingcompany.blogspot.com

Robin Krall
208.573.4398
Lipstickgypsy1965@hotmail.com
Lipstick-gypsy.blogspot.com

Robuck Antiques on 6th Street
Jenifer Robuck
1808 W. 6th St.
Austin, TX 78703
512.419.1112
jenner@prismnet.com

Roll'en Hills Moving and Delivery
281.204.7434
www.rollenhillsmoving.com

Ruby Rose
1335 Walker St.
San Luis Obispo, CA 93401
805.545.7964
Rubyrose805.com
Rubyrose805@gmail.com

Rust in Peach
Tony McCray
404.944.5533
Facebook.com/tonymccray.rustinpeace

Sacred Heart Antiques
Jessica Fairbrother
615 S. Church St.
Tupelo, MS 38804
662.352.3027
sacredheartantiques@yahoo.com

Sarah Smith Salvage Style
239.246.4267
theglobalswapshop.com
smithsalvage@yahoo.com

Scottsdale Marketplace
Home & Garden
6310 N. Scottsdale Rd.
Scottsdale, AZ 85253
480.368.5720
scottsdalemarketplace.com

Serenite Maison
Alexandra Cirimelli
4149 Old Hillsboro Rd.
Leiper's Fork, TN 37064
615.599.2071
serenitemaison.com
Serenitemaison@bellsouth.net

Southwestern Elegance
P.O. Box 1447
Ingram, TX 78025
830.367.4749

southwesternelegance.com
southwesternelegance@gmail.com

Stash Style
440.364.4923
www.stashstyle.com

Sue's Gift World
103 County Rd.
Clifton, TX 76634
254.622.8446
Suebid1@embarqmail.com

Susan Wheeler Home
5515 Airport Way S.
Seattle, WA 98108
360.402.5080
susanwheelerhome.com
susan@susanwheelerhome.com

Sweet Salvage
4648 N. 7th Ave.
Phoenix, AZ 85013
602.279.2996
Sweetsalvage.net

The Good Stuff
248.390.6063
Nancyrose32@yahoo.com

The Red Barn—The Original
Susan and Bo Franks
P.O. Box 180
Smithville TX 78957
512.13.3562
info@roundtoptexasantiques.com

The Vintage Round Top
1450 N Hwy. 237
Round Top, TX 78954
713.859.5993
info@thevintageroundtop.com
thevintageroundtop.com

The Willows
3743 E. Indian School Rd.
Phoenix, AZ 85018
602.334.1345
willowshomeandgarden.com
willowdesign@gmail.com

The Texas Rose Antique Show
2075 S. State Hwy. 237
Round Top, TX 78954
256.390.5337
texasroseshow.com
info@texasroseshow.com

Bull Chic Antiques
Blue Hills Antique Show
979.208.9141
bullchicantiques.com

Tobacco Road Primitives
Marburger Farm Antique Show
Round Top, TX 78954
678.576.4539
Tobaccoroad98@yahoo.com

Traveler's Market
Lesley Anne Martin
153B Paseo De Peralta
Santa Fe, NM 87501
505.989.7667
www.travelersmarket.net
Lesley@pacificartefacts.com

Twenty Six Twenty
2620 Joanel St.
Houston, TX 77027
713.840.9877

Utopia
Jacqui Stoneman, Harry J. Myers
3812 Mockingbird Ln.
Dallas, TX 75205
214.443.9999
harrymyers@aol.com

Vincent Peach
533 Church St., Ste. 359
Nashville, TN 37203
615.378.1374
www.vincentpeach.com
info@vincentpeach.com

Vintage Sculpture
By Brad and Sundie Ruppert
5190 Fulton St.
Norwalk, IA 50211
515.865.3943
Vintagesculpture.com
vintagesculpture@studiogonline.com